C000185171

COUNTRYSIDE
CONTEMPLATIONS

REFLECTIONS ON OUR WILD WONDERS

TRIGGER
The mental health & wellbeing publisher

Published in Great Britain 2020 by Trigger Publishing
Originally published as The Countryside Companion in Great Britain
2005 by Robson Books
Trigger is a trading style of Shaw Callaghan Ltd
& Shaw Callaghan 23 USA, INC.
The Foundation Centre
Navigation House, 48 Millgate, Newark
Nottinghamshire NG24 4TS UK
www.triggerpublishing.com
British Library Cataloguing in Publication Data
A CIP catalogue record for this book is available upon request
from the British Library
ISBN: 9781789561883
This book is also available in the following eBook formats:
ePUB: 9781789561890
Cover design by stevewilliamscreative.com
Typeset by stevewilliamscreative.com
Printed and bound in Great Britain by CPI Group (UK) Ltd,
Croydon CR0 4YY
Paper from responsible sources

CONTENTS

ON LANDSCAPE

To the lost man, to the pioneer penetrating a new country, to the naturalist who wishes to see the wild land at its wildest, the advice is always the same – follow a river. The river is the original forest highway. It is nature's own Wilderness Road.

EDWIN WAY TEALE, naturalist

There is pleasure in the pathless woods,

there is rapture in the lonely shore,

there is society where none intrudes,

by the deep sea, and music in its roar;

I love not Man the less,

but Nature more.

LORD BYRON, poet

The hot day is the first day of summer. The day when you realise that there can be too much sunshine, the day when the heat strikes up from bare soil and reflects back from walls and buildings, the day, above all others, when you can truthfully say, 'Thank goodness I am not in a town.'

RALPH WIGHTMAN, farmer and broadcaster

PAUSE FOR THOUGHT

What a scene was that corn-field under the hot August sky! Fiery red glowed the faces of the harvestmen, against the golden background, a sea of waving wheat, the famed ruddy-hued wheat of Talavera. Not a cloud obscured the burning blue heavens, whilst beyond the standing corn showed here and there a bit of foliage, lofty hedge starred with wild roses or low pollard oaks of deep rich green.

As the afternoon drew on the sultriness increased, and these brilliant contrasts of colour grew more intense. Southern warmth and gorgeousness seemed to invest that Suffolk harvest field. But the bucolic mood of the reapers had passed. As the sickles moved automatically backwards and forwards, not a word passed their lips, a regiment of deaf mute were hardly quieter. From time to time, at a signal of the leader, each stood up, wiped his brow, shook himself, took a draught of beer, interchanged a word with his fellow, then resumed work vigorously as before.

The sun sank behind the pollard oaks and twilight succeeded, hardly bringing coolness. A little later, although no breeze sprang up, pleasant freshness lightened their labours; another and yet another drink from the master's can lent new strength, long after moon rising, that mechanical swing of twenty arms, that gleam of twenty sickles went on. Deep, almost solemn silence reigned over

the corn-field. Only the rustle of footsteps and wheat falling on the stover broke the stillness, a stillness and monotony emblematic of these noiseless, unheroic lives, the tide of human existence that perpetually ebbs and flows, leaving no memory behind.

MATILDA BETHAM EDWARDS, The Lord of the Harvest, (1899)

Here and elsewhere we shall not obtain the best insight into things until we actually see them growing from the beginning.

ARISTOTLE

The clearest way into the Universe is through a forest wilderness.

JOHN MUIR, naturalist

POINT OF INTEREST

The New Forest is no such thing. It is neither new
(it was created by William the Conqueror in the
eleventh century), nor is it a forest as we know
the term today. In Norman England a forest was an
area of land outside usual jurisdiction, giving the king
the right to do pretty much whatever he pleased
with it. What pleased William was to dispose of the
various settlements, farms and villages in that area
of Hampshire, and stock the land with deer. If there
was anything William liked it was a good hunt. As one
twelfth century chronicler, Orderic Vitalis, wrote: 'So
great was his love of woods that he laid waste more
than 60 parishes, forced the peasants to move to
other places, and replaced the men with beasts of the
forest so that he might hunt to his heart's content'.

If anyone was looking to get revenge for this deed, it came in the most ironic of ways. William's second son, Richard, was killed in a hunting accident in the forest, as was his third son, William Rufus, and his grandson, another Richard. The sins of the fathers..."

Should you shield the canyons from the wind storms you would never see the true beauty of their carvings.

ELISABETH KUBLER-ROSS, psychiatrist

I chanced to rise very early one particular morning this summer, and took a walk into the country to divert myself among the fields and meadows, while the green was new, and the flowers in their bloom. As at this season of the year every lane is a beautiful walk, and every hedge full of nosegays, I lost myself, with a great deal of pleasure, among several thickets and bushes that were filled with a great variety of birds, and an agreeable confusion of notes, which formed the pleasantest scene in the world to one who had passed a whole winter in noise and smoke. The freshness of the dews that lay upon everything about me, with the cool breath of the morning, which inspired the birds with so many delightful instincts, created in me the same kind of animal pleasure, and made my heart overflow with such secret emotions of joy and satisfaction as are not to be described or accounted for.

JOSEPH ADDISON, Essay (1672-1719)

There is a serene and settled majesty to woodland scenery that enters into the soul and delights and elevates it, and fills it with noble inclinations.

WASHINGTON IRVING, author

It is not so much for its beauty that the forest makes a claim upon men's hearts, as for that subtle something, that quality of air that emanation from old trees, that so wonderfully changes and renews a weary spirit.

ROBERT LOUIS STEVENSON, author

So they went on and into the silence of the wood. The soft warmth brooded over it – the winds were still. High up in the beeches spots of red gold were widening slowly, and the acorns showed thickly on the oaks. Then past narrow 'drives', or tracks going through the woods, bounded on each side with endless walls of ash-poles with branches of pale green; carpeted with dark green grass and darker moss luxuriating in the dank shade, and roofed with spreading oakspray. These vistas seemed to lead into unknown depths of forest. They paused and looked down one, feeling an indefinite desire of exploration; and as they looked, in the silence a leaf fell, brown and tanned with a trembling rustle, and they saw its brown oval dot the rank green grass, upon whose blades it was upborne. On again, and out into a broad glade, where the rabbits had been at play, and raced to their hiding places. Here were clumps of beeches, brown with innumerable nuts; straight grown Spanish chestnuts, with spiny green balls of fruit; knotted oaks; and tall limes, already yellow and filled by the sunshine with a hazy shimmer of colour. Over the glade a dome of deep-blue sky, and warm loving sun, whose drowsy shadows lingered and moved slow. After a while they reached the hazel-bushes, acres upon acres of them; tall straight rods, with tapering upturned branches, whose leaves fell in a shower when the stem

was shaken. Nuts are the cunningest of fruit in their manner of growth; outwardly they show a few clusters fairly enough, especially bunches at an almost inaccessible height; when these are gathered, those who are not aware of the ways of the hazel naturally pass on, leaving at least twice as many unseen. The nuts grow under the bough in such a position that, in pulling it down to reach a visible bunch, the very motion of the bough as it bends hides the rest beneath it. These will stay till they drop from the hoods, till, turning to a dark and polished brown, they fall rattling from branch to branch to the earth. There again the dead brown leaves hide them by similarity of colour. So that, to thoroughly strip a hazel-bush requires a knowledge of the likely places and the keenest of eyes.

RICHARD JEFFERIES, Greene Ferne Farm, (1880)

Why, one day in the country Is worth a month in the town

CHRISTINA ROSSETTI, poet

PAUSE FOR THOUGHT

Three days later, when we arrived in the Highlands, everything seemed too beautiful to be true. But that is an ungrateful thing to say: better to exclaim with Emily Dickinson, 'O matchless earth! We underrate the chance to dwell in thee!'

A matchless bit of earth it appeared that afternoon as we drove the five long miles from the station to our cottage. So quiet it all was, that a door might have been shut in the sky between the turmoil of London and the vaulted stillness of this great valley. In the limpid atmosphere every crumple on the flanks of the distant hills was visible, and the creaking axle of our old carriage made the only sound. As we came nearer to the mountains, a delicate shrillness crept into the puffs of scented wind. It revived the very soul, after weeks of the stifling atmosphere of town.

MARY AND JANE FINDLATER, Content with Flies, (1916)

The country is lyric, the town dramatic. When mingled, they make the most perfect musical drama.

HENRY WADSWORTH LONGFELLOW, poet

All art is but imitation of nature.

LUCIUS ANNAEUS SENECA, philosopher

PAUSE FOR THOUGHT

Nowhere else does the greater light so rule the day, so measure, so divide, so reign, make so imperial laws, so visibly kindle, so immediately quicken, so suddenly efface, so banish, so restore, as in a plain like this of Suffolk with its enormous sky. The curious have an insufficient motive for going to the mountains if they do it to see the sunrise. The sun that leaps from a mountain peak is a sun past the dew of his birth; he has walked some way towards the common fires of noon. But on the flat country the uprising is early and fresh, the arc is wide, the career is long. The most distant clouds, converging in the beautiful and little-studied order of cloud-perspective (for most painters treat clouds as though they formed perpendicular and not horizontal scenery), are those that gather at the central point of sunrise.

On the plain, and there only, can the construction – but that is too little vital a word; I should rather say the organism – the unity, the design of the sky be understood. The light wind that has been moving all night is seen to have not worked at random. It has shepherded some small flocks of cloud afield and folded others.

There's husbandry in Heaven. And the order has, or seems to have, the sun for its midst. Not a line, not a curve, but confesses its membership in a design declared from horizon to horizon.

ALICE MEYNELL, The Rhythm of Life and Other Essays, (1893)

For me, a landscape does not exist in its own right, since its appearance changes at every moment; but the surrounding atmosphere brings it to life – the light and the air which vary continually. For me, it is only the surrounding atmosphere which gives subjects their true value.

CLAUDE MONET, artist

ON COUNTRY LIFE

A wealthy landowner cannot cultivate and improve his farm without spreading comfort and well-being around him. Rich and abundant crops, a numerous population and a prosperous countryside are the rewards for his efforts.

ANTOINE LAVOISIER, chemist

It was a perfect day

For sowing; just

As sweet and dry was the ground

As tobacco-dust.

I tasted deep the hour

Between the far

Owl's chuckling first soft cry

And the first star.

A long stretched hour it was;

Nothing undone

Remained; the early seeds

All safely sown.

And now, hark at the rain,

Windless and light,

Half a kiss, half a tear,

Saying good-night.

EDWARD THOMAS, Sowing

Nature has spread for us

a rich and delightful banquet.

Shall we turn from it?

THOMAS COLE, artist

PAUSE FOR THOUGHT

I shall never forget those early days in the fields; that was my first experience at real work. Old Launcelot had sent down to the school for boys and girls to help with the haymaking. I was one of those chosen to go forth and put my shoulder to the wheel, or my hand to the implement. About all I really did do, though, was to lead the horses, carry the wooden bottles of ale to and from the farm, or rake up the hay with the girls; but I felt very important, especially when the time came round to receive my wages for the task – a bright two-shilling piece every week-end. How strong the sun shone in the meadows! How strange and far off the hills looked to be! And how beautiful the trees, and copses, and hedges were to my boyish eyes! I can still see the far-off corn-fields quivering with the heat, the near meadows trembling too, the tall elms like spectres, everything in nature stock still, as though it were painted so; not a breath of air, not a sound but the tinkle of the mowing machine half a mile away, the rattle of the waggons, the voices of the pitchers and loaders, and the young girls laughing and talking as they raked away behind...

How different it all was from the long dragging day, the smoke, and filth, and fume, the foul stench and suffocating dust and atmosphere of the factory! The sweat of the open fields is clean and sweet, yielded naturally; that of the other place, before

the furnace, is wrung from your very heart and soul in anguish, leaving you faint, weary, powerless, and exhausted. The other is gentle, medicinal, corrective, and salutary.

ALFRED WILLIAMS, A Wiltshire Village, (1912)

Nature is painting for us, day after day, pictures of infinite beauty, if only we have the eyes to see them. The earth has received the embrace of the sun and we shall see the results of that love.

SITTING BULL, Lakota chief

Those who contemplate the beauty of the earth find reserves of strength that will endure as long as life lasts. There is something infinitely healing in the repeated refrains of nature—the assurance that dawn comes after night, and spring after winter.

RACHEL CARSON, biologist

PAUSE FOR THOUGHT

The night was of a Cimmerian blackness. In the tree-tops the wind raved like a demented thing. All round me, as I felt my way along with my feet, a thousand little rivulets splashed and gurgled in the deep of the woods.

But I was not long in striking Slumberwell. The lane plunged down into what seemed interminable forest, then brought up short on a spit of grassland, which, next morning, I discovered to be the village-green.

Friendly lights beamed out at me from all sides; and as I stopped outside one of the largest houses, there sounded overhead a familiar creaking and groaning, which I knew to be an inn-sign battling with the breeze.

That evening I spent by the tap-room fire, in an old oak settle; with the landlord's slippers on my feet; the jovial, white-haired landlord himself at my elbow; the landlady, in curl-papers and spectacles, sewing by the light of a tallow candle hard by; and a wonderful old man and his son, to complete the company. Others dropped in from time to time, and dropped out again; but we five made up the enduring elements of the scene. We took it in turn to keep the talk going, and the process was surprisingly easy. Each in turn related some simple experience, the simpler the better, provided it was wrapped about with numberless little details

and unimportant etceteras, and spun out to its last reach. The old ploughman was especially great at this gentle exercise, and held our little circle spell-bound for a whole ten minutes while, for instance, he related how he had succeeded in stopping a pig.

TICKNER EDWARDES, Lift-luck on Southern Roads, (1990)

It's only the urban middle-class who worry about the preservation of the countryside, because they don't have to live in it.

SIR HUMPHREY APPLEBY, fictional character

PAUSE FOR THOUGHT

I have lately myself been moved to ask: why are the villages sleepy? Why are they stagnant, lifeless places of at most an antiquarian interest, where the picturesque tourist wanders about looking, often in vain, for the church-key? There can be no doubt of the answer. It is because the best young men all go away. There is no inducement for them to remain.

The country-side is continually being drained of its best blood. The reason villages are sleepy is because the farm labourers are wretchedly paid, miserably housed, and insufficiently fed. I confess to some impatience in reading in the daily press of a prize won by a farm labourer and his wife at the Lincoln Agricultural Show for bringing up a large family on low wages. People should not be encouraged to do this; they should be incited to demand higher wages. It was not stated what the prize was; possibly a sovereign. It was won by bringing up fifteen children on fifteen shillings a week ... If the day ever comes when these people, fed on gruel and bread with or without dripping, are called on to defend their hearths and homes – I ask our Imperialist friends to consider the point – they will probably put up a very poor fight.

RL GALES, The Vanished Country Folk, (1914)

When one tugs at a single thing in nature, he finds it attached to the rest of the world.

JOHN MUIR, naturalist

POINT OF INTEREST

A good candidate for The Worst Farmer Ever must be the young man who, back in the mid-seventeenth century, was taken out of school by his mother to run the family farm. He was hopeless. Once, when he was supposed to be watching the livestock, he was found curled up under a hedge with a good book. Another time when he was supposed to be taking the produce to market, he was seen trying jumping experiments, to determine how forceful the wind was.

By the time his mother gave up on him, she'd lost some of the cattle, and no-one knew where the eggs were. But at least he had a full notebook of scribblings, including recipes for clearing the brain, a formula for making chalk, observations about the stars above, and a method for making gold ink.

The young man's name was Isaac Newton.

New Zealand is not a small country but a large village.

PETER JACKSON, director

It is pure unadulterated country life. They get up early because they have so much to do and go to bed early because they have so little to think about.

OSCAR WILDE, poet

For any stranger who might have a fancy for seeing the Welsh people in the hours of ease, no better stage could be selected than the shady walks which converge on the pump-room at Llanwrtyd.

Five or six times a day, before and after every meal, the long procession of patients and holiday-makers traverses the half mile of road which connects the village and the Dolecoed grounds where they mostly disport themselves.

All ages and almost all classes are represented in the motley concourse that, increasing with each July day, keeps up such a regular promenade. Half of them, perhaps, are chattering Welsh and all of them, save a few cripples, are as garrulous and happy as they ought to be when the cares of farm and mine, of pulpit, shop and office are cast aside. Here is a Baptist preacher waving his croquet mallet at his fellow players with much of that authority which the pulpit has made a second nature, and oblivious for the time of local politics or the disestablishment of the Church. There is a country parson from North Wales bursting with information on Church statistics and interested in the price of sheep. Here again is a group of young men singing part songs as they stroll along with as much nonchalance and accuracy as if they had imbibed the art with their mothers' milk; there a

bench full of Cardiganshire farmers talking chapels and crops, any one of whom would be painfully disconcerted if called upon at a moment's notice for a complete sentence of English. The Mothers of Wales are here too of course with their knitting, those capacious, determined looking matrons I have so often alluded to with unstinted admiration. What a fine holiday it must be for them too, chickens and milkcows, calves and pigs, wash tubs and sewing machines, all abandoned for a whole blessed fortnight, or even for a month. No woman in the world must surely enjoy a change quite so thoroughly as a working farmer's wife!

A.G. BRADLEY, Highways and Byways in South Wales, (1914)

Whoever makes two ears of corn, or two blades of grass to grow where only one grew before, deserves better of mankind, and does more essential service to his country than the whole race of politicians put together.

JONATHAN SWIFT, author

It was near [a] copse that in early spring I stayed to gather some white sweet violets, for the true wild violet is very nearly white.

I stood close to a hedger and ditcher, who, standing on a board, was cleaning out the mud that the water might run freely. He went on with his work, taking not the least notice of an idler, but intent upon his labour, as a good and true man should be. But when I spoke to him he answered me in clear, well chosen language, well pronounced, 'in good set terms'.

No slurring of consonants and broadening of vowels, no involved and backward construction depending on the listener's previous knowledge for comprehension, no half sentences indicating rather than explaining, but correct sentences. With his shoes almost covered by the muddy water, his hands black and grimy, his brown face splashed with mud, leaning on his shovel he stood and talked from the deep ditch, not much more than head and shoulders visible above it.

It seemed a voice from the very earth, speaking of education, change, and possibilities.

RICHARD JEFFERIES, Nature near London, (1883)

Agriculture not only gives riches

to a nation, but the only riches she can

call her own.

SAMUEL JOHNSON, poet

Heaven is under our feet as well as over our heads.

HENRY DAVID THOREAU, essayist

PAUSE FOR THOUGHT

It is a lovely day during the last week in May. There has been no rain for more than a fortnight; the wind is north-east, and the sun shines brightly, yet we walk down to the River Coln, anticipating a good day's sport among the trout: for, during the may-fly season, no matter how unpropitious the weather may appear, sport is more of a certainty on this stream than at any other time of year.

Early in the season drought does not appear to have any effect on the springs; we might get no rain from the middle of April until half-way through June, and yet the water will keep up and remain a good colour all the time. But after June is 'out', down goes the water, lower and lower every week; no amount of rain will then make any perceptible increase to the volume of the stream, and not until the nights begin to lengthen out and the autumnal gales have done their work will the water rise again to its normal height. If you ask Tom Peregrine why these things are so, he will only tell you that after a few gales the 'springs be frum'. The word 'frum', the derivation of which is, Anglo-Saxon, 'fram', or 'from' = strong, flourishing, is the local expression for the bursting of the springs.

Our friend Tom Peregrine is full of these quaint expressions.

When he sees a covey of partridges dusting themselves in the roads, he will tell you they are 'bathering'. A dog hunting through

a wood is always said to be 'breveting'... The ground on a frosty morning 'scrumps' or feels 'scrumpety' as you walk across the fields; and the partridges when wild are 'teert'. All these phrases are very happy, the sound of the words illustrating exactly the idea they are intended to convey.

J. ARTHUR GIBBS, A Cotswold Village, (1898)

If you live according to nature, you never will be poor; if according to the world's caprice, you will never be rich.

PUBLILIUS SYRUS, author

ON NATURE

Nature! We are surrounded and embraced by her: powerless to separate ourselves from her...

T.H. HUXLEY, biologist

When silver snow decks Sylvio's clothes

And jewel hangs at shepherd's nose,

We can abide life's pelting storm

That makes our limbs quake,

if our hearts be warm.

Whilst Virtue is our walking-staff

And Truth a lantern to our path,

We can abide life's pelting storm

That makes our limbs quake,

if our hearts be warm.

Blow, boisterous wind, stern winter frown,

Innocence is a winter's gown;

So clad, we'll abide life's pelting storm

That makes our limbs quake,

if our hearts be warm.

WILLIAM BLAKE, Song by an Old Shepherd, The Good Life

I roamed the countryside searching for answers to things I did not understand. Why thunder lasts longer than that which causes it, and why immediately on its creation the lightning becomes visible to the eye while thunder requires time to travel. How?

LEONARDO DA VINCI, artist

PAUSE FOR THOUGHT

It was joyful to hear the merry whistle of blackbirds as they darted from one clump of greenery to the other. Now and again a peaty amber colored stream rippled across their way, with ferny over-grown banks, where the blue kingfisher flitted busily from side to side, or the gray and pensive heron, swollen with trout and dignity, stood ankle-deep among the sedges. Chattering jays and loud wood-pigeons flapped thickly overhead, while ever and anon the measured tapping of Nature's carpenter, the great green woodpecker, sounded from each wayside grove.

ARTHUR CONAN DOYLE, The White Company, (1891)

Nature understands no jesting; she is always true, always serious, always severe; she is always right, and the errors and faults are always those of man.

JOHANN WOLFGANG VON GOETHE, author

Live in each season as it passes; breathe the air, drink the drink, taste the fruit, and resign yourself to the influence of the earth.

HENRY DAVID THOREAU, essayist

PAUSE FOR THOUGHT

Welcome sweet Aprill! thou gentle Midwife of May's Pride, and the Earth's green Livery. Methinks I heare the little sweet birds making ready their warbling Accents ready to entertaine the Rising Sun and welcome him from the Antipodes and those remoter Regions that have all this winter rob'd us of his comfortable beames and benigne influence. But now the Cuckoe is come and the laborious Bees look about for honey. The Nightingale begins to tune her melodious throat against May: and the Sunny showers perfume the Aire. The Dew hangs in Pearles upon the tops of the grasse; while the Turtles sit billing on the little gree boughs. The beasts of the Wood look out into the plaines: and the Fishes out of the deep run up into the shallow waters. The Fowls of the Aire begin to build their Nests and sencelesse Creatures gather life into their bodyes. The Sun with his refulgent rayes enlightens and warmes the Aire, and the little Flyes to Flock and swarme in it. Now the Muses try the Poetasters in the Pamflets. Time is now gracious in Nature, and Nature in time.

MATTHEW STEVENSON, The Twelve Moneths, (1661)

Keep a green bough in your heart and a singing bird will come.

LAO TZU, philosopher

Home to us was not a fireside, nor even father and mother and brothers and sisters, but included a village, wide grass fields, spinneys dotted among them, a moat and a brook, all populous with very familiar denizens, whether two-legged or four-legged or six-legged; and as time went on and incidents accumulated, spinney, pond, field, tree, and the rest were written over with a quite unforgettable script.

SIR WILLIAM BEACH THOMAS, war correspondent

Nature understands no jesting; she is always true, always serious, always severe; she is always right, and the errors and faults are always those of man.

JOHANN WOLFGANG VON GOETHE, author

POINT OF INTEREST

Climate change is happening, and year upon year it's becoming more dramatic. How it will affect our landscape and environments is difficult to predict, because the natural responses to the change will depend upon the exact pace of the warming of our climate. But results so far suggest that species are already on the move and altering their usual patterns.

Daffodils have been flowering as early as Christmas Day, and oak trees have come into leaf three weeks earlier than they did in the 1950s. Grass now grows all year round, and a few reports have come in, even from Scotland, of grass that needed mowing in winter. And, of course, the humble bee is declining rapidly.

These changes will affect local ecosystems, which in turn affect landscapes and environments. Beech woods, for example, may struggle to respond to the different

seasonal timings of what is going on around them, and steadily start to disappear. Similarly, the agricultural pockets of East Anglia might become too dry to farm effectively, shifting the farming centre of the UK further west and north, and changing the landscape forever.

If we could see the miracle of a single flower clearly, our whole life would change.

BUDDHA

Let children walk with Nature, let them see the beautiful blendings and communions of death and life, their joyous inseparable unity, as taught in woods and meadows, plains and mountains and streams of our blessed star, and they will learn that death is stingless indeed, and as beautiful as life.

JOHN MUIR, naturalist

In the winter time the Rat slept a great deal, retiring early and rising late. During his short day he sometimes scribbled poetry or did other small domestic jobs about the house; and, of course, there were always animals dropping in for a chat, and consequently there was a good deal of story-telling and comparing notes on the past summer and all its doings.

Such a rich chapter it had been, when one came to look back on it all! With illustrations so numerous and so very highly coloured! The pageant of the river bank had marched steadily along, unfolding itself in scenepictures that succeeded each other in stately procession. Purple loosestrife arrived early, shaking luxuriant tangled locks along the edge of the mirror whence its own face laughed back at it. Willow-herb, tender and wistful, like a pink sunset cloud, was not slow to follow. Comfrey, the purple hand-in-hand with the white, crept forth to take its place in the line; and at last one morning the diffident and delaying dog-rose stepped delicately on the stage, and one knew, as if string-music had announced it in stately chords that strayed into a gavotte, that June at last was here. One member of the company was still awaited; the shepherd-boy for the nymphs to woo, the knight for whom the ladies waited at the window, the prince that was to kiss the sleeping summer back to life and love. But when meadow-

sweet, debonair and odorous in amber jerkin, moved graciously to his place in the group, then the play was ready to begin.

KENNETH GRAHAME, The Wind in the Willows, (1908)

Keep your love of nature, for that is the true way to understand art more and more.

VINCENT VAN GOGH, artist

That best of diaries is one which is referred to, perhaps, more often at the end of the year, when one season's records and occurrences are being compared with another's, than at any other time. There is a quiet charm in turning the closely printed pages and scanning a chronicle which is all of open air and simple country detail. The very names of the common weeds and insects of the summer countryside take on added graces under the grey skies and behind the drawn curtains of December. 'Wild carrot flowers', you read, and you are back in the spacious sunshine of June; or a note on the burnet moth takes you among the flowers and grasses of hayfields still uncut.

ERIC PARKER, In Wind and Wild, (1909)

I wonder if the snow loves the trees and fields, that it kisses them so gently? And then it covers them up snug, you know, with a white quilt; and perhaps it says 'Go to sleep, darlings, till the summer comes again.'

LEWIS CARROLL, author

The sun, with all those planets revolving around it and dependent upon it, can still ripen a bunch of grapes as if it had nothing else in the universe to do.

GALILEO, astronomer

PAUSE FOR THOUGHT

Not until I went out could I tell that it was softly and coldly raining. Everything more than two or three fields away was hidden. Cycling is inferior to walking in this weather, because in cycling chiefly ample views are to be seen, and the mist conceals them. You travel too quickly to notice many small things; you see nothing save the troops of elms on the verge of invisibility. But walking I saw every small thing one by one; not only the handsome gateway chestnut just fully dressed, and the pale green larch plantation where another chiff-chaff was singing, and the tall elm tipped by a linnet pausing and musing a few notes, but every primrose and celandine and dandelion on the banks, every silvered green leaf of honeysuckle up in the hedge, every patch of brightest moss, every luminous drop on a thorn tip. The world seemed a small place: as I went between a row of elms and a row of beeches occupied by rooks, I had a feeling that the road, that the world itself, was private, all theirs; and the state of the road under their nests confirmed me. I was going hither and thither to-day in the neighbourhood of my stopping place, instead of continuing my journey.

EDWARD THOMAS, In Pursuit of Spring, (1914)

Let anyone who possesses a vivid imagination and a highly-wrought nervous system, even now, in this century, with all the advantages of learning and science, go and sit among the rocks, or in the depths of the wood, and think of immortality, and all that that word really means, and by-and-by a mysterious awe will creep into the mind, and it will half believe in the possibility of seeing or meeting something – something – it knows not exactly what.

RICHARD JEFFERIES, author

And this, our life, exempt from public haunt, finds tongues in trees, books in the running brooks, sermons in stones, and good in everything.

WILLIAM SHAKESPEARE, poet and playwright

ON FOLKLORE

"Among the scenes which are deeply impressed on my mind, none exceeded in sublimity the primeval forests undefaced by the hand of man.

CHARLES DARWIN, naturalist

The shepherds idle hours are over now

Nor longer leaves him neath the hedgrow bough

On shadow pillowd banks and lolling stile

Wilds looses now their summer friends awhile

Shrill whistles barking dogs and chiding scold

Drive bleating sheep each morn from fallow fold

To wash pits where the willow shadows lean

Dashing them in their fold staind coats to clean

Then turnd on sunning sward to dry agen

They drove them homeward to the clipping pen

In hurdles pent where elm or sycamore

Shut out the sun – or in some threshing floor

There they wi scraps of songs and laugh and tale

Lighten their anual toils while merry ale

Goes round and gladdens old mens hearts to praise

The thread bare customs of old farmers days

JOHN CLARE, The Shepherds Calendar – June

A seed hidden in the heart of an apple is an orchard invisible.

WELSH PROVERB

PAUSE FOR THOUGHT

The Devil never keeps his bargains. Many years ago he struck one with a Devonshire brewer named Frankan, who, it is said, was alarmed at the effect the new cult of cider-drinking was having on his trade. So he sold his soul to the Devil in return for frosts on May 19th, 20th and 21st sufficiently hard to ruin the apple-blossom. In recent years the Devil has been observing his side of the contract only half-heartedly; in 1978 and again in 1980 he ignored it entirely.

Everywhere the trees were loaded, with branches splitting under the weight of fruit. The gales of early September littered the ground beneath the trees with fallen fruit, yet the crop left on the trees still seemed undiminished.

RALPH WHITLOCK, The Countryside: Random Gleanings, (1982)

I might mention all the divine charms of a bright spring day, but if you had never in your life utterly forgotten yourself in straining your eyes after the mounting lark, or in wandering through the still lanes when the fresh opened blossoms fill them with a sacred silent beauty like that of fretted aisles, where would be the use of my descriptive catalogue?

GEORGE ELIOT, author

When the bird and the book disagree,

believe the bird.

JOHN JAMES AUDUBON, ornithologist

PAUSE FOR THOUGHT

The English claim him as their own, as do the Scots and the Welsh. There are some who would have him as Roman. But now there's a theory that Arthur, that great rural king, was in actual fact Russian.

The thinking is that the Sarmatians, a nomadic group who made their way from Central Asia to Europe, finally ended up in Britain in the second century as workers for the Romans. A warrior race, skilled with swords and on horseback, they were used to guard Hadrian's Wall, and their tales of derring-do may well have been passed on to the Anglo-Saxons. Intriguingly, there is a race of people today in the Russian Caucasus – the Ossetians – who are descended from the Sarmatians, and who tell tales of a king with a magic sword who followed a chalice of truth. Even the name Excalibur is thought by the same theorists possibly to have derived from a Greek word for a group of famous blacksmiths, the Kalybes, who once lived where the Ossetians live today.

Every particular in nature, a leaf, a drop, a crystal, a moment of time is related to the whole, and partakes of the perfection of the whole.

RALPH WALDO EMERSON, essayist

Should you come across a wishing well, you'll need to do more than just chuck in a coin and hope for the best. Tradition states that you should stoop and drink from the palm of your hand three times, without speaking, while running the wish through your mind. You must never divulge your desire to anyone, or disaster is likely to strike. Singing your wish is most definitely a mistake. The disaster aspect comes about because most wishing wells are associated with a religious figure, most likely a saint, with whom you make a silent pact while drinking the water, a pact that you must not break.

One example of such a well on the Isle of Man was written about by Juan Othigill in the Manx Quarterly, Issue nine in 1910: 'The celebrated well on Maughold Head is situated half-way down the face of the cliff sloping to the sea, and like most holy wells, is formed in shape like a horseshoe.

Tradition has it that it represents the imprint of the hoof of St. Patrick's steed, when he took a flying leap across the Island — the healing and magic waters gushing forth as a 'testimony to the virtues of the message of good tidings that he carried with him.'

Nature never deceives us. It is we who deceive ourselves.

JEAN-JACQUES ROUSSEAU, philosopher

POINT OF INTEREST

The novel *Watership Down* by Richard Adams not only introduced the world to the trek by Hazel, Fiver, Bigwig and all from Berkshire to Hampshire, but revealed once and for all that rabbits have a religion.

It appears that Frith, the Sun God, created the earth and the stars from his droppings. The creatures lived off the grass that Frith provided, but the great god noticed one day that the family of El-ahrairah, the rabbit prince, were eating all the grass by themselves.

Warning the prince that he needed to keep his family under control, Frith was angered when the rabbit replied that his people would do what they wished, as they were the best in the world. Frith therefore gave the other families – the foxes, badgers, stoats and so on – the ability to eat rabbits, sending El-ahrairah off in a panic.

But Frith is not a heartless god – he also gives the rabbit the gift of powerful hind legs to help him run from his many enemies.

It's all true, you know.

A tree does not move unless there is wind.

AFGHAN PROVERB

There are no words that can tell the hidden spirit of the wilderness, that can reveal its mystery, its melancholy, and its charm.

THEODORE ROOSEVELT, former US President

PAUSE FOR THOUGHT

The blackthorn has had a chequered background when it comes to superstitions, variously seen as a holy tree in medieval times, and as a symbol of evil. It was the pure white blossom that appeared on leafless branches that gave it its heavenly connotations, while the darkness of its bark simultaneously suggested an association with more demonic ways. Some even believe that Christ's crown was fashioned from its twigs, and in some parts of England, it was fashioned into the shape of a crown, burnt, and then its ashes scattered across crop fields to encourage a good harvest.

It is also considered unlucky to bring blackthorn into the house – unless you lived in Hertfordshire, in which case a scorched crown of the plant, hung up on New Year's morning, brought good luck.

All in all, it's a plant as convoluted in folklore as its twisted branches make it in the hedgerows.

Nature, whose sweet rains fall on unjust and just alike, will have clefts in the rocks where I may hide, and secret valleys in whose silence I may weep undisturbed.

OSCAR WILDE, poet

PAUSE FOR THOUGHT

An old folktale explaining the true origin of the Wrekin, the 1,334 foot high hill standing on the Shropshire plain:

There was once a wicked old giant in Wales, who had been banished there by the people of Shrewsbury and had developed a very great spite against them. As the years passed since his banishment, he steadily planned his revenge, and finally came up with an idea: he would dam the Severn, and cause such a flood that the town would be drowned.

So off he set, carrying a mighty spadeful of earth, tramping along mile after mile trying to find his way back to Shrewsbury. But so many years had it been since last he was there, he had forgotten the route.

He went some way off course, and found himself eventually at Wellington, tired and confused, and beginning to lose interest in his great plan. He did not realise how close to Shrewsbury he was.

Sitting by the side of the road to get his breath back, he espied a man coming down the road towards him. It was a cobbler with a sack of old boots and shoes strung on his back, who was from Wellington, and who once a fortnight walked to Shrewsbury to collect his customers' old boots and shoes, and take them home with him to mend.

The giant called out to him. 'I say, how far is it to Shrewsbury?'

'Shrewsbury?' replied the cobbler. 'What do you want at Shrewsbury?'

'I want to fill up the Severn with this lump of earth I've got here' he answered. 'I've an old grudge against the mayor and the folks at Shrewsbury, and I mean to drown them and get rid of them all at once.'

The cobbler considered this, and realised it would not do. He could not afford to lose all his customers in this way, so thinking quickly, he undid his sack.

'Look at these' he said to the giant, showing him the old boots he was carrying. 'I've come from Shrewsbury myself, and I've worn these out on my march'.

The giant moaned. 'Oh, then it's no use. I'm exhausted already, and can't carry this load of mine any further.' And so saying, he dropped the earth on the ground just where he stood, scraped his boots with his spade, turned on his heel, and was never seen again.

And where he put down his load stands the Wrekin to this day. And by its side stands the little Ercall, made from the earth he scraped off his boots.

If you look deep enough you will see music; the heart of nature being everywhere music.

THOMAS CARLYLE, historian

Everything has beauty, but not everyone sees it.

CONFUCIUS, philosopher

PAUSE FOR THOUGHT

The best of the countryside's donkey beliefs, (one or two are rather asinine):

- Wear the hairs from a donkey's back in a charm around your neck to guard against whooping cough and toothache. The dark mark on the animal's spine is said to have appeared after it bore Christ into Jerusalem.
- If your mare is pregnant, set a black donkey into the field with her, and she won't miscarry.
- If you see a dead donkey, good luck will come your way – particularly if you jump over the body three times.
- Having said that, you're unlikely to see one. Donkeys were believed to know when they were about to die, and hide themselves away.
- A braying donkey that twitches its ears foretells rain.
- If your child is sick, ride a donkey backwards, facing the tail end.

To see a world in a grain of sand and heaven in a wild flower, hold infinity in the palm of your hand and eternity in an hour.

WILLIAM BLAKE, poet

We want to help you to not just survive but thrive ... one book at a time

Find out more about Trigger Publishing by visiting our website:

triggerpublishing.com

or join us on:

Twitter @**TriggerPub**

Facebook @**TriggerPub**

Instagram @**TriggerPub**

A proportion of profits from the sale of all Trigger books
go to their sister charity, The Shaw Mind,
founded by Adam Shaw and Lauren Callaghan.
The charity aims to ensure that everyone has access
to mental health resources whenever they need them.

Find out more: **shawmindfoundation.org**

or join them on:

Twitter: @**Shaw_Mind**

Instagram: @**Shaw_Mind**

LinkedIn: @**shaw-mind**

FB: @**shawmindUK**